FINDING WAKÂ
SUNFLOWER'S STORY

The Publisher: Eschia Books Inc.

Library and Archives Canada Cataloguing in Publication
Title: Sunflower's story / by Sunflower Paul ; illustrator, Chloe "Bluebird"
Mustooch.
Names: Paul, Sunflower, author.
Description: Series statement: Finding Wakâ
Identifiers: Canadiana (print) 20190199660 | Canadiana (ebook)
20190199911 | ISBN
9781926696843 (softcover) | ISBN 9781926696850 (EPUB)
Subjects: LCSH: Paul, Sunflower. | LCSH: Paul, Sunflower—Mental
health. | LCSH: Indigenous peoples—Suicidal behavior—Canada—
Prevention. | CSH: Native peoples—Canada—Rites and ceremonies. |
CSH: Native peoples—Canada—Biography. | CSH: Native peoples—
Suicidal behavior—Canada—Prevention.
Classification: LCC E98.R53 P38 2020 | DDC 299.7/131—dc23

Project Director: Dianne Meili
Cover Image: Chloe "Bluebird" Mustooch
Illustrations: Chloe "Bluebird" Mustooch
Cover Design: Gregory Brown

Stony Plain Public Library acknowledges it is in Treaty
6 territory, the traditional territory of the Plains Cree,
Woodland Cree, Beaver Cree, Saulteaux, Niisitapi
(Blackfoot), Métis, and Nakota Sioux Peoples.

Produced with the assistance of the Government of Alberta.

We acknowledge the financial support of the Government of Canada.
Nous reconnaissons l'appui financier du gouvernement du Canada.

Funded by the Government of Canada
Finance par le gouvernement du Canada

PC: 39-1

FINDING WAKÂ

SUNFLOWER'S STORY

by Sunflower Paul

Illustrated by Chloe "Bluebird" Mustooch

ESCHIA BOOKS

My name is Sunflower, and I'm from Alexis Nakota Sioux Nation, west of the city of Edmonton in Alberta, Canada. My people are related to the great Sioux Nation in the United States. My parents and my family have always been involved in ceremony, and I have helped at these gatherings since I was small.

My great grandmother named me "Sunflower" when I was born. She was a special person in my life. When I was little, I helped my grandmother cook for the people coming to ceremonies. I was the "Tree Girl" in a Sundance when I was only six years old.

As the Tree Girl at the Sundance ceremony, I blessed the sacred tree of the Sundance lodge before it was cut down. I prayed with the tree and spent four days in ceremony. This is a tradition that has begun the Sundance ceremony for hundreds of years among my Nakota people.

For as long as I can remember, I helped my grandmother prepare for ceremonies. We were always together in the kitchen, making food for our people to eat when they gathered to pray.

My grandmother taught me so much. I learned how to cut strips of wild game to make dried meat. The knife you use is sharp so you can cut thin slices that will dry evenly. I cut myself a few times, but it was worth it to know how to make the drymeat everyone loves to eat.

When you are a spiritual person and you trust in *Wakâ,* you understand that the Spirits are always there to help you, even if you can't always see them. When we say *Wakâ* in our Nakota Sioux language, it means the Great Mystery, who created everything. We can't explain how it works because it is not for our human minds to know. The things that other people call "miracles" happen because the Creator knows you are a good person, and beings in the Spirit World bless you.

But when I was in grade eight, I forgot about *Wakâ* and really began to doubt myself when I became part of a blended family. My mom's new husband, Clifford, moved from the city with his kids into our home, and let's just say we didn't all get along.

My mom wanted all of us kids to attend school in the city, and that meant I had to leave my old school on the rez. Every day, Clifford drove six of us into Edmonton. That meant a cramped hour and a half drive from Alexis.

This might not sound so bad, but imagine stuffing yourself into a small car, with six other people, some of whom you don't even really know. It's either five in the morning, and the sun isn't up yet, or it's five in the evening, and the sun is down. Everyone is tired and cranky. You are sitting there, shoulder to shoulder, and your slightest move bothers the one beside you. Then after the endless trip into the city, you get dropped off at a crowded school instead of the one that you've known all your life in your home community.

Things had been fine in my house with my older and younger brothers and sisters, but that all changed when my stepfather and his kids moved in. Right from the start, I had problems with my stepsister Rebecca. She was two years younger than me; she was spoiled and she talked too much. I know she didn't like the new situation any more than I did.

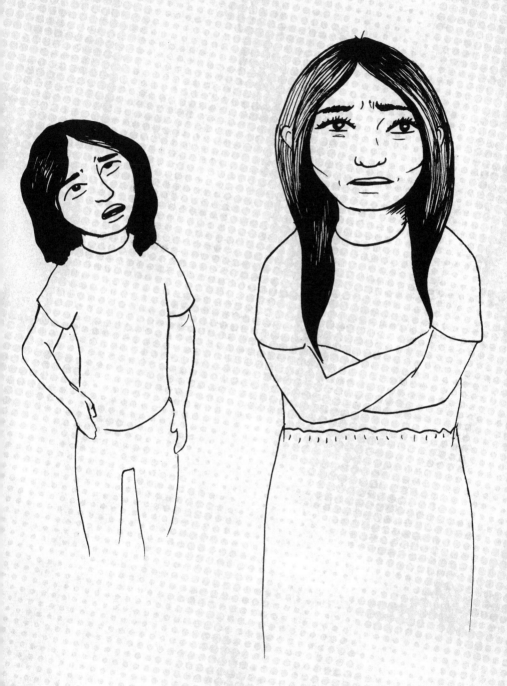

It wasn't as if I could get away from her either. There was always that long drive to school on weekdays. I was stuffed into the car with my stepdad Clifford, Rebecca, Lucy, Tiffany, Daniel and Karen. That's seven people! We had to drop kids off at different schools, and it took forever. Everybody was cranky, and things just got worse when winter came. The roads were icy, and the trip took even longer.

I was so stressed out, and I got angry fast. I felt like everyone in the world had it in for me. I thought my mom moved back to the rez with her husband and all his kids just to make my life miserable.

I have always been a pretty patient person, but one morning when I was sitting next to Rebecca, I lost it. I can't even remember what she did or said, but I hauled off and hit her. She whacked me back, and we got into a huge fight. The other kids were scared, and my stepdad was really mad. We couldn't wait to get out of the car.

The bad feelings between the adults and kids in my family got worse and worse. There were arguments all the time.

Then, to make things worse, one morning we got into a car accident. The jolt of the other car slamming into us terrified me. After that, I would clench my teeth and stiffen up whenever my stepdad jammed on the brakes or a car passed too close. I know now that I was suffering from Post-Traumatic Stress Disorder.

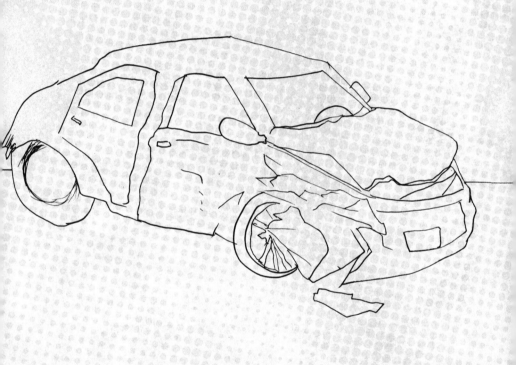

I felt uneasy about everything and didn't trust anyone. I believe the body IS connected to the mind because my negative thinking became physical pain. My chest began to ache horribly, but I didn't tell anyone about it, hoping it would just go away. I finally told my teachers when I started getting anxiety attacks at least twice a week. They tried to help me and told me I could walk out of class if we were talking about a subject that might make me uncomfortable, like death or suicide. They thought difficult topics bothered me and brought on my chest pain, but that wasn't it. I didn't want to attract attention to myself, so I just stayed in class.

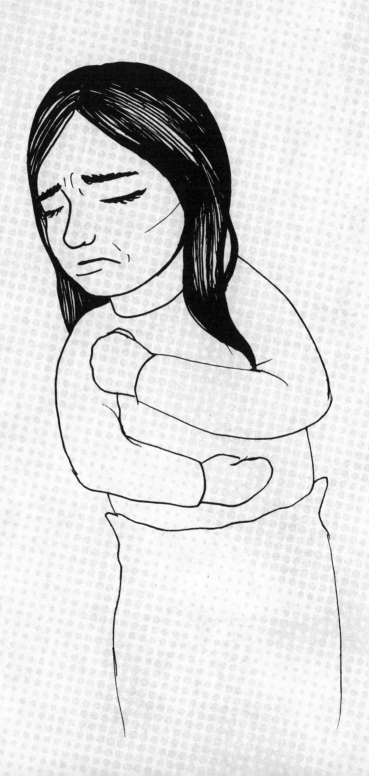

Besides my stepsister Karen, who was the same age as me, I didn't know anyone in the city school. Most of the white kids were mean to me because I was an "Indian." Those kids showed me how ugly racist behaviour is.

As the year went on, I started to feel like an outsider at home and school. I was sad and edgy all the time, and I didn't feel like I belonged anywhere. I started to think no one cared whether I lived or died.

In January of that year, my mom moved out of our rez house. She wanted me to stay in my city school to finish grade eight, so that meant living at my uncle's house in Edmonton. My brother moved in, too. He and my uncle were not the cleanest people. Being a girl, I was expected to clean up after them. That totally sucked! Even worse was the loneliness. I didn't like being alone for five days, and I only got to go home on the weekends.

Around the time I was staying with my uncle, my older sister wasn't coming home. I worried about her. I thought something bad was going to happen to her and that she would become another missing or murdered Indigenous woman.

My life was out of control and so was my stress. I wondered why I cared so much about my family and other people when they didn't seem to care about me. I decided I cared too much. But the anxiety was still getting me down. On really bad days, when I was really struggling, I thought about ending the craziness. I thought about suicide, but I didn't make a plan or start giving my stuff away. I knew suicide wasn't the answer.

Deep down, I understood I was on this earth for a reason. I knew the Creator had gifted me with a loving heart, and I really wanted to help myself and others.

Ever since I was a little girl, I'd heard people talking about the power of fasting out on the land. I heard how people would go off by themselves to spend time alone, going without food or water to pray for help from the Spirits.

I talked to my Grandpa Willard about fasting, and he told me what he knew. He said our people entered into a fast in the springtime, after the first thunder sounded, which meant the Thunder Beings had returned from the west and were here to help. He said I needed to have a good reason to fast and be serious about what I was doing.

"In your fasting place, you are going to want food and water," Grandpa Willard told me. "You will want to come out of the sweat lodge to eat and drink. You may fear the darkness and what comes at night. But go beyond the needs of your body and move into a place of Spirit where you begin to know your higher self, the real unlimited you, beyond all of the small things of the world."

There was a lot to get ready before the day finally came when I would spend 24 hours in a dark, covered sweat lodge, without food or water. My grandfather showed me how to make prayer ties. I prayed for what I needed as I put tobacco into the middle of white, yellow, red and black cloth squares.

The four colours are the sacred colours of my Nakota people. I tied the squares into little bundles, and I had to string the bundles together—all 405 of them—and make sure the string didn't twist. Praying, alone and in the quiet, I went within myself and got more in touch with my inner Spirit than I had for a long time.

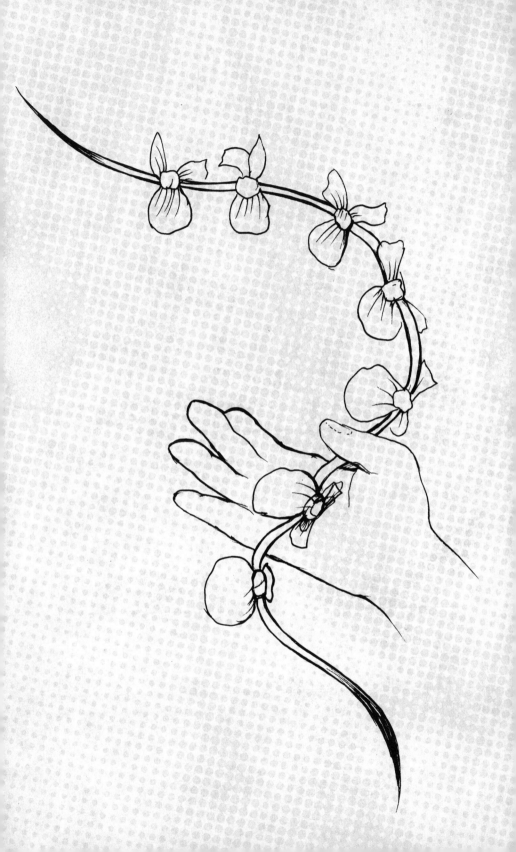

Before I went into the sweat lodge, my grandfather got me whatever I wanted to eat. I asked for pizza, and after my last bite, I wondered how I would handle being hungry.

In my sacred place, my grandfather showed me how to fill my grandmother's pipe with red willow bark shavings and tobacco. It was such a good feeling to use the sacred pipe that she uses when she prays.

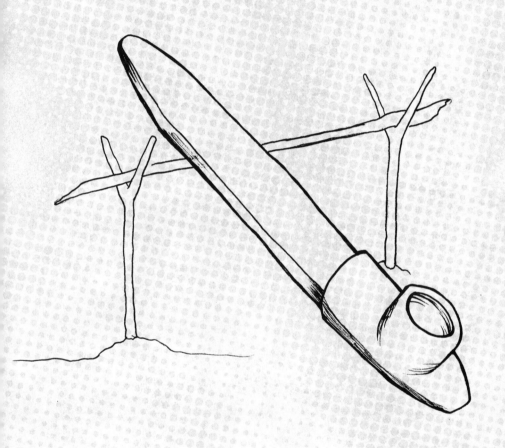

The sweat lodge was made from fresh, bent willow branches covered with canvas. My grandfather said it would be the "womb" from which I would be "reborn," washed clean of the thoughts and feelings I no longer needed or wanted. The lodge was on my Grandpa Charlie's Sundance grounds where it is clean, and there are no power poles or electricity nearby. It was a peaceful, powerful place, and I felt good there.

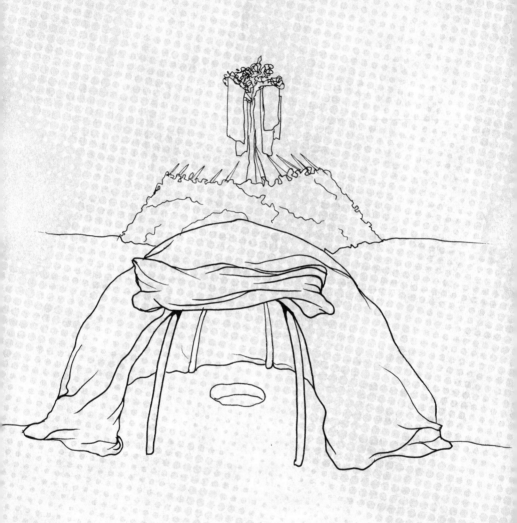

Inside the lodge, I didn't see or hear anything. Everything was quiet. I began to relax and release my anxious thoughts and tense muscles. I lost track of time.

I can't explain how I felt during my fast. I can only say I felt like I was somewhere else. Eventually, I fell asleep. When I woke up, I felt different. Something had been lifted from me. Maybe *Wakâ*, the Great Mystery, had smoothed the way for me. I felt stronger, and I knew that I would never be alone. There will always be positive and negative in my life, but I understand that things like gossip or racist comments cannot really harm me anymore because I am stronger than that.

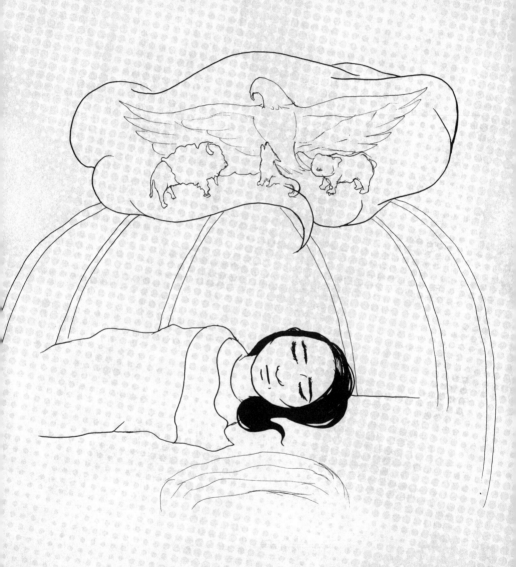

Over time I realized what had happened. The fast had given me a little push down a different road. It lifted me up and opened my eyes to the beauty of this world and all of the positive things surrounding me. My life was a gift to enjoy, and I didn't have to suffer through it. I realized the Creator, my community and my family—especially my grandfather—are always there to help. I always have ceremony to come back to when I need to be reminded I am pure spirit, connected to everything.

I'm ready to graduate from grade 12, and I have a job at the store in my community. People, especially my mom, are so proud of me. I can accomplish whatever I put my mind to.

Trusting in our traditional Nakota Sioux teachings has helped me to stay humble, and I am proud of what I can do to help others. As an Indigenous woman, these traditions are a part of me. I can walk in the modern world with an education and gain strength and guidance from my traditions as a Nakota person as I move through my amazing life.

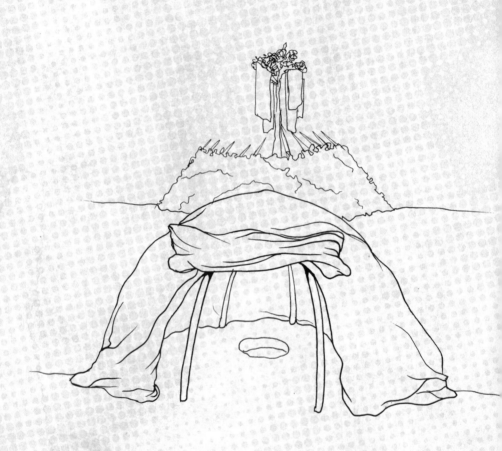